THE ILLUSTRATED
ENCYCLOPEDIA

VOLUME 5

J - M

Belitha Press

First published 1995 by
Macmillan Education Australia Pty Ltd

First published in the United Kingdom in 1995 by
Belitha Press Limited
31 Newington Green, London N16 9PU

Cataloguing in print data available from the British Library.

ISBN 1 85561 524 X (Vol 5)
ISBN 1 85561 529 0 (Set)

Consultant: Frances Warhurst
UK editor: Maria O'Neill
Project editor: Jo Higgins

Typeset by Polar Design
Printed in Hong Kong

Acknowledgements

The author and publisher are grateful to the following for permission to reproduce copyright photographs:

Cover: Coo-ee Picture Library

Air-France, p. 9 (top left); Kevin Aitken/A.N.T. Photo Library, p. 51 (bottom); Australian Picture Library, p. 60 (bottom);
M. Cermak/A.N.T. Photo Library, p. 34; Coo-ee Picture Library, pp. 10, 11, 16, 13, 19, 20 (top), 23 (top right), 24, 26 & 27, 29
(right), 31, 33 (top), 35 (bottom), 37 (left), 38, 40, 41 (bottom), 48, 51 (top right & bottom left), 55 (top left), 63 (bottom), 64;
Nigel Dennis/A.N.T. Photo Library, p. 5 (centre & bottom right); General-Motors Holden, p. 31 (bottom right); Hazelton
Airlines, p. 9 (bottom); International Picture Library, p. 53; Japan Information Centre, p. 63 (top); Gerard Lacz/A.N.T. Photo
Library pp. 5 (bottom), 33 (centre); MIM Holdings, pp. 43 (right), 50 (left); NASA, pp. 58 (bottom), 58 & 59; NHPA/A.N.T.
Photo Library, pp. 33 (bottom), 44 (left), 54 (top right); Northern Territory Tourist Commission, p. 22; Northside
Photographics, pp. 8, 21, 39, 45, 47 (top right), 49, 61 (top); The Photo Library, pp. 20 (bottom), 25; QANTAS Australia, p. 9
(top right); Otto Rogge/A.N.T. Photo Library, pp. 18 (right), 23 (top); Silvestris/A.N.T. Photo Library, pp. 5 (top & centre), 26
(left); Ron & Valerie Taylor/A.N.T. Photo Library, p. 7 (bottom right); J. Weigel/A.N.T. Photo Library, p. 44 (right); Norbert
Wu/A.N.T. Photo Library, p. 7 (top).

While every care has been taken to trace and acknowledge copyright the publishers tender their apologies for any accidental
infringement where copyright has proved untraceable.

Illustrators
Sharyn Madder: 4, 5, 10, 11, 14, 17, 32, 33, 54, 55,
Rhyll Plant: 6, 7, 18, 19, 22, 23, 48, 51, 63
John Fairbridge: 12, 13, 15, 16, 25, 30, 31, 45, 46, 47, 52, 53, 58, 59, 62, 64
Paul Konye: 8, 9, 20, 21, 28, 29, 37, 39, 42, 43, 49, 60, 61
Andrew Plant: 26, 27, 34, 35, 40, 41, 44
Xiangyi Mo: 26 (top), 36
Chantal Stewart: 38, 56, 57

HOW TO USE THIS BOOK

The Illustrated Encyclopedia has over 300 entries. The entries are arranged alphabetically. To find your topic, use the guide letters at the top of each page to check you have the right volume. The first letter of your topic will be highlighted.

TOPIC: JELLYFISH

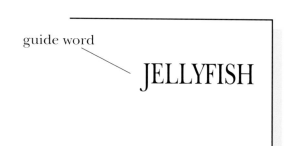

guide letter

A B C D E F G H I J K L M

Use the guide words printed in the top right-hand corner of each page to find your topic. The guide words list the entries on a double-page spread. They are listed alphabetically. Check the guide words to see if you need to go backwards or forwards.

guide word

JELLYFISH

You can also use the index in Volume 9 to find your topic.

jellyfish
Volume 4   61
Volume 5   **6–7**

If you cannot find your topic in its alphabetical order in the encyclopedia, use the index.

Jupiter
see planet

TOPIC: JUPITER

The index lists all the topics in alphabetical order. It tells you where you will find your topic.

More information on how to use the encyclopedia and the index can be found in Volume 9.

JAGUARS AND LEOPARDS

SEE ALSO
• Animal • Cat • Lion
• Mammal

Jaguars and leopards belong to the wild cat family. A jaguar looks like a leopard, but it is heavier and stronger. Both animals are excellent hunters.

PARTS OF A JAGUAR

Average length: 2.5 metres including tail
Average weight: 130 kilograms

ears can turn in any direction to hear sounds

yellow fur with black spots

keen eyesight for hunting

nose – keen sense of smell

sensitive whiskers

tail

strong legs for climbing

WHERE JAGUARS AND LEOPARDS LIVE

Jaguars
● Central America
■ South America

Leopards
◆ Asia
★ Africa

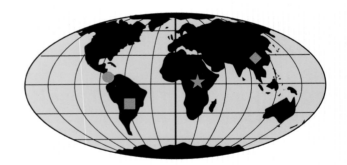

JAGUARS' AND LEOPARDS' FUR

Jaguars and leopards have fur which camouflages them. Their fur has many black spots. The spots are arranged in small circles or rosettes.

• A jaguar's fur has a spot in the middle of each rosette.

• A leopard's fur does not have a spot in the middle of each rosette.

JAGUARS AND LEOPARDS

FOOD

Jaguars and leopards eat other animals. They are carnivores.

Jaguars eat:

capybaras   peccaries

tapirs   wild pigs

deer   fish

alligators

Leopards eat:

antelopes   goats

dogs   monkeys

sheep   snakes

PANTHERS ▶
Black leopards are often called panthers. They are so dark you can hardly see their spots.

HOW LEOPARDS LIVE
• Leopards climb trees easily. They sleep in trees. A leopard often drops on its prey from a tree. If it cannot eat all its food at once, it will drag the dead animal up into a tree, so lions and hyenas cannot eat it.
• A female leopard gives birth to two to four cubs at a time. The cubs feed on their mother's milk. The mother looks after her cubs until they can hunt for themselves.

HOW JAGUARS LIVE
• Most jaguars live and hunt alone. They stalk their prey. When they kill a large animal, they often drag it away – sometimes even up a tree.
• A female jaguar gives birth to two to four cubs every two years.

CONSERVATION
In the past, jaguars and leopards have been hunted for their fur. Today, many countries have agreed not to trade in jaguar and leopard fur and to protect the places where they live.

5

JELLYFISH

SEE ALSO
• Animal • Coral
• Invertebrate

A jellyfish is a sea animal. Most jellyfish are bell shaped with long, trailing tentacles. Jellyfish have hollow bodies. They do not have a skeleton.

PARTS OF A JELLYFISH

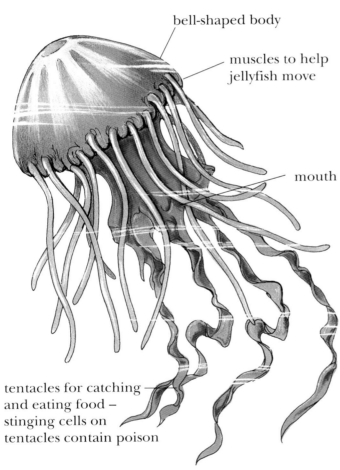

bell-shaped body

muscles to help jellyfish move

mouth

tentacles for catching and eating food – stinging cells on tentacles contain poison

Size: up to 2 metres wide

SAFE FROM DANGER ▶
Some small fish are not harmed by jellyfish stings. They can hide from their enemies in a jellyfish's tentacles.

WHERE JELLYFISH LIVE

Jellyfish usually live in warm, shallow seas. You can see them floating near the surface of the water.

COLOUR
Some jellyfish are transparent. Others are tinted blue, pink, mauve, yellow or brown.

INTERESTING FACT
Jellyfish get their name from their jelly-like bodies.

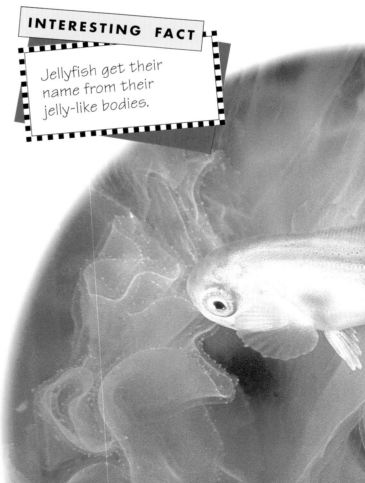

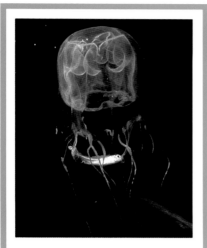

HOW JELLYFISH MOVE

Jellyfish float in the water with their tentacles trailing below. They swim by contracting and expanding their bell-shaped bodies.

FOOD

Most jellyfish eat small sea animals. Jellyfish use their tentacles to paralyse small animals.

small fish   prawns

HOW JELLYFISH LIVE

- Eggs are fertilized and develop into larvae.
- Tiny larvae grow into polyps.
- The polyps divide into segments and develop into adults.

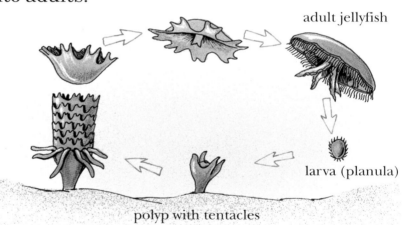

adult jellyfish

larva (planula)

polyp with tentacles

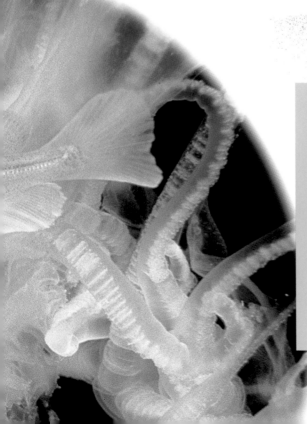

DANGEROUS JELLYFISH

The box jellyfish is one of the most deadly jellyfish in the world. It is found in tropical waters.

JET ENGINE

SEE ALSO • Airport • Aeroplane • Transport

A jet engine is pushed forwards by a jet of hot gases shooting backwards. Most aeroplanes are powered by jet engines.

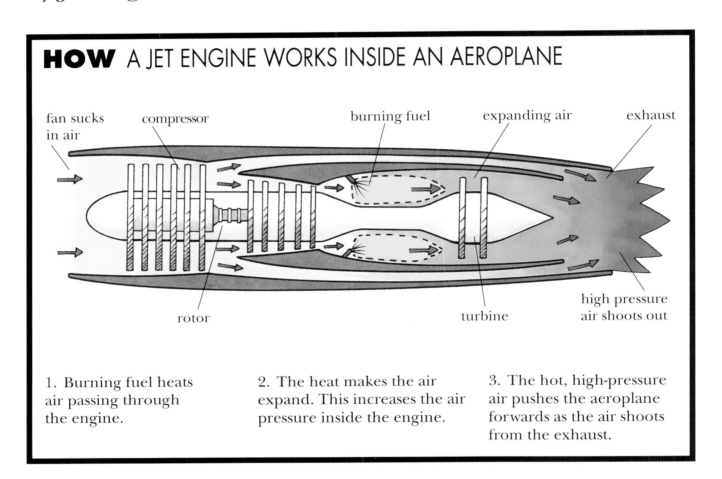

HOW A JET ENGINE WORKS INSIDE AN AEROPLANE

fan sucks in air

compressor

burning fuel

expanding air

exhaust

rotor

turbine

high pressure air shoots out

1. Burning fuel heats air passing through the engine.

2. The heat makes the air expand. This increases the air pressure inside the engine.

3. The hot, high-pressure air pushes the aeroplane forwards as the air shoots from the exhaust.

A JET-POWERED BALLOON

Blow up a balloon and let it go. The jet of air escaping backwards from the neck makes the balloon fly through the air.

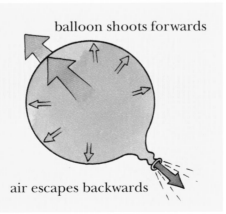

balloon shoots forwards

air escapes backwards

INTERESTING FACT

The first jet aeroplane to fly was made in Germany in 1939.

KINDS OF JET ENGINES

Turbojet engines ▲ are used in supersonic aeroplanes.

Turboprop engines ▶ turn a propeller. Many small fast aeroplanes have a turboprop engine.

Turbofan engines ▲ have fans at the front to push air back into the engines. Many airliners such as Boeing 747 are powered by these engines.

A JUMBO JET

Jumbo jets are large passenger aeroplanes driven by jet engines.

The pilot, copilot and flight engineer fly the jumbo from the cockpit.

Flight attendants work on aeroplanes to assist passengers.

Meals are prepared in the galley.

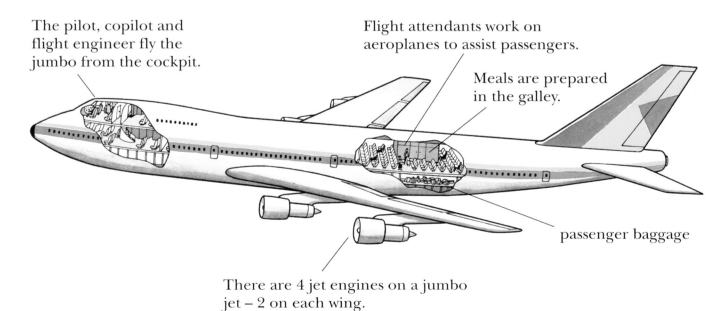

passenger baggage

There are 4 jet engines on a jumbo jet – 2 on each wing.

KANGAROO

SEE ALSO
• Animal • Mammal
• Marsupial

A kangaroo is a marsupial. Marsupials are a group of animals that carry their young in a pouch. Kangaroos can hop on their back legs.

PARTS OF A KANGAROO

ears for keen hearing

eyes for keen sight

short, soft fur

nose for smelling danger

sharp teeth for grazing

short front legs mainly for grasping food

sharp claws to defend itself against enemies

powerful back legs for hopping and leaping

tail

Average height: 2 metres
Average weight: 66 kilograms

HOW KANGAROOS MOVE

Kangaroos can leap and hop great distances. They can travel over 40 kilometres per hour.

TAILS

A kangaroo's tail is used as:
• a balance when hopping and moving slowly
• a prop when standing.

WHERE KANGAROOS LIVE

● **Australia**
■ **New Guinea**

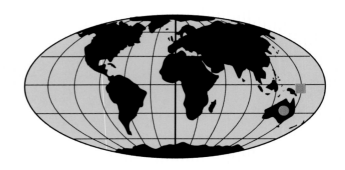

HOW KANGAROOS LIVE

• A joey only partly develops inside its mother. At birth, it crawls into its mother's pouch and feeds on her milk.
• At nine months, the joey leaves the pouch for short periods.
• A joey may stay in its mother's pouch until it is about 18 months old.

A male kangaroo is called a buck. A female kangaroo is called a doe. A young kangaroo is called a joey.

Most kangaroos live in groups called mobs. Some kangaroos live alone. Kangaroos graze in open forest, woodland and grassland. Some live in rain forests, while others live in deserts.

FOOD

Kangaroos eat plants. They are herbivores.

A WALLABY

A wallaby is similar to a kangaroo, only smaller.

KITE

SEE ALSO • Air • Hang-gliding • Hobby • Toy

A kite is a toy that can fly. It has a light frame which is covered with material. When wind lifts the frame, the kite flies.

PARTS OF A FLAT, DIAMOND-SHAPED KITE

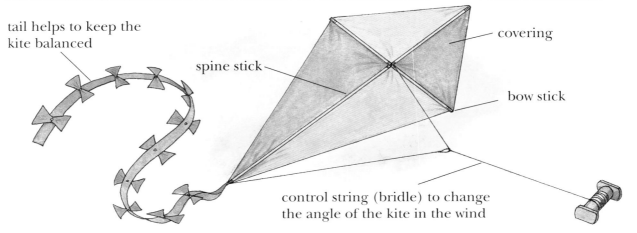

tail helps to keep the kite balanced

spine stick

covering

bow stick

control string (bridle) to change the angle of the kite in the wind

HISTORY

The first kites were made in China about 3000 years ago. They were made from bamboo frames covered with silk.

INTERESTING FACT

A hang-glider is like a giant kite.

HANDY HINTS FOR KITE FLYING

• Kites fly best in light or moderate wind.
• Choose a large open area in which to fly your kite.
• Make sure there are no electric poles, towers or overhead wires nearby.
• Wind the string around something to protect your hands.

KITE FLYING

People of all ages can enjoy flying kites. Kite flying is a popular sport. Kite flyers need lots of practice to become champions.

KINDS OF KITES

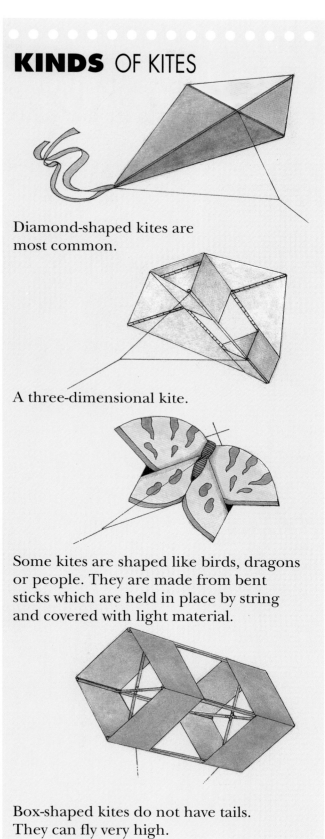

Diamond-shaped kites are most common.

A three-dimensional kite.

Some kites are shaped like birds, dragons or people. They are made from bent sticks which are held in place by string and covered with light material.

Box-shaped kites do not have tails. They can fly very high.

KIWI

SEE ALSO • Animal • Bird

A kiwi is a type of bird that cannot fly. It lives in forests in New Zealand.

PARTS OF A KIWI

long beak for searching and catching food

dull brown, soft hair-like feathers

small wings

nostrils at tip of beak to smell and find food

short neck

Length: 35 to 46 centimetres

FOOD

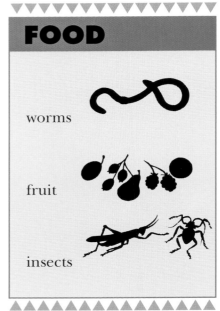

worms

fruit

insects

WHERE KIWIS LIVE

● **New Zealand**

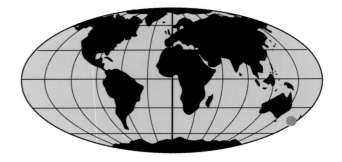

HOW KIWIS LIVE

• Kiwis sleep during the day. They come out at night to hunt for food.
• They build nests in burrows.
• The female lays up to two large eggs. The male sits on the eggs and waits until they hatch. The eggs take about 11 weeks to hatch.

KNIGHT

SEE ALSO • Archery • Castle • Heritage

A knight was a warrior who fought on horseback. Knights fought for kings and queens during the Middle Ages. In return, they were given land and became rich and powerful.

A KNIGHT OF THE MIDDLE AGES

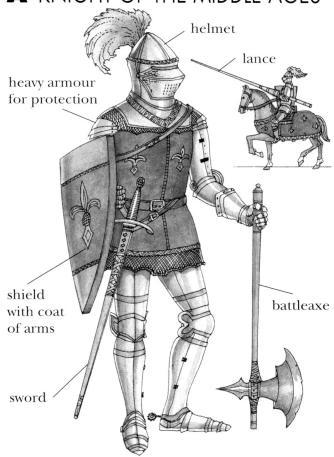

helmet

lance

heavy armour for protection

shield with coat of arms

battleaxe

sword

Each knight had a different coat of arms so others could recognize him.

A KNIGHT'S TRAINING

Only boys from rich families could become knights. They were trained by another knight or lord.

- A boy served as a page from seven years of age. Pages learned the rules of being a knight and how to fight.
- At 15, a page became a squire. Squires learned how to fight on horseback. They helped their master in battle.
- At 21, a squire could become a knight.

page   squire   knight

HISTORY

In the 1500s, guns were first used in battle. A knight's armour no longer protected him. Knights were no longer effective warriors.

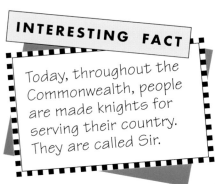

INTERESTING FACT

Today, throughout the Commonwealth, people are made knights for serving their country. They are called Sir.

15

KNOT

SEE ALSO • Boat • Sailing • Yacht

A knot is a way of tying rope, string or thread. Knots can be used to tie up a parcel, join two ends together or make a loop in a rope.

KINDS OF KNOTS

There are many different kinds of knots.

A granny knot is the one most people use. It is not a strong knot.

A reef knot is for joining two ends together. Sailors use reef knots.

A bowline knot is used to make a loop at the end of a rope. It is useful for tying up animals.

The sheepshank is used to shorten a rope without cutting it. A sheepshank can also make a weak part of a rope stronger.

Two half hitches can be used to tie a rope to a post quickly.

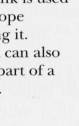

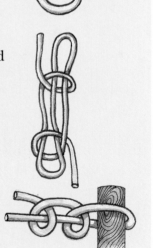

USES OF KNOTS

People have used knots for hundreds of years. They have been used to make many different things.

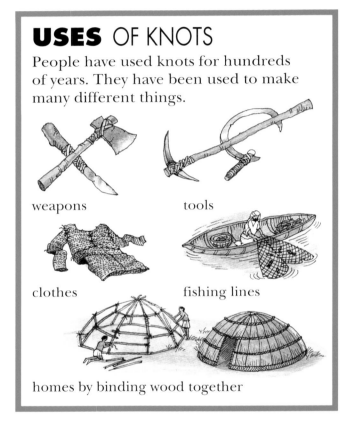

weapons

tools

clothes

fishing lines

homes by binding wood together

Sailors, fishermen and climbers use knots to help them.

16

KOALA

A koala is a marsupial. It spends most of its life in eucalyptus trees.

SEE ALSO
• Endangered Species
• Mammal • Marsupial

PARTS OF A KOALA

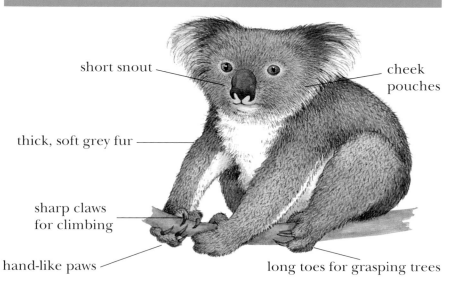

short snout

cheek pouches

thick, soft grey fur

sharp claws for climbing

hand-like paws

long toes for grasping trees

Average height: 75 to 80 centimetres

WHERE KOALAS LIVE

● **South-eastern and east coast of Australia**

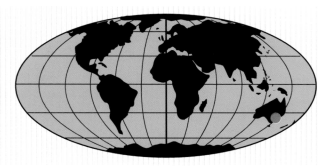

FOOD

Koalas only eat certain kinds of eucalyptus leaves.

CONSERVATION

Koalas have become an endangered species. In the past, koalas have been hunted for their fur. Many have also been killed by bushfires, disease and forest clearing.

HOW KOALAS LIVE

• Koalas usually live alone. They sleep about 18 hours each day. They feed late in the afternoon and at night.

• A female koala has one baby a year. At birth, a young koala is small and only partly developed. It crawls to its mother's pouch and stays there for six months.

• A young koala feeds on its mother's milk.

17

LADYBIRD

SEE ALSO • Animal • Beetle • Insect

A ladybird is a small, round beetle.
Ladybirds are brightly coloured with spots.

PARTS OF A LADYBIRD

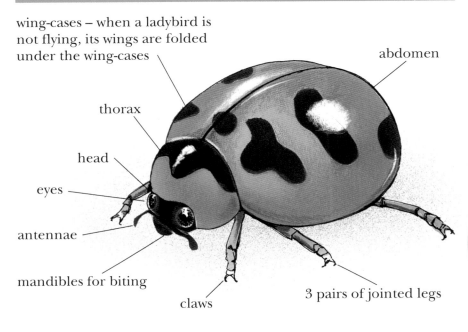

wing-cases – when a ladybird is
not flying, its wings are folded
under the wing-cases

abdomen

thorax

head

eyes

antennae

mandibles for biting

claws

3 pairs of jointed legs

COLOURS OF LADYBIRDS

Some ladybirds are red or
yellow with black, red, white
or yellow spots. The bright
colours warn enemies that
ladybirds do not taste good.

LIFE CYCLE OF A LADYBIRD

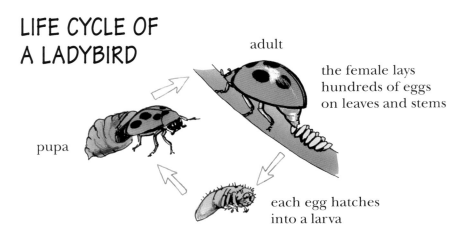

adult

the female lays
hundreds of eggs
on leaves and stems

pupa

each egg hatches
into a larva

USEFUL INSECTS

Ladybirds eat insects which are harmful to crops.

FOOD

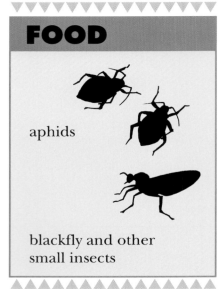

aphids

blackfly and other
small insects

LAKE

SEE ALSO
• Dam • Glacier • Irrigation
• River • Water

A lake is a large area of water surrounded by land. Some lakes are freshwater ones. Other lakes are saltwater ones.

HOW GLACIAL LAKES FORM

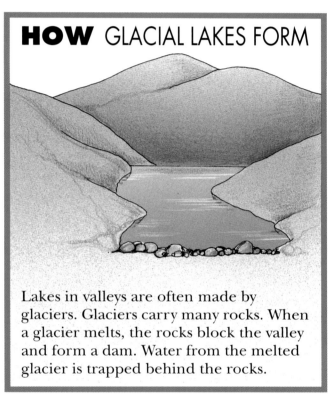

Lakes in valleys are often made by glaciers. Glaciers carry many rocks. When a glacier melts, the rocks block the valley and form a dam. Water from the melted glacier is trapped behind the rocks.

LOCH NESS ▼

In Scotland, there is a myth that a huge monster lives in a lake called Loch Ness.

INTERESTING FACT

Some seas are really lakes. The world's largest lake is the Caspian Sea. It is a saltwater lake.

THE ECOSYSTEM OF A FRESHWATER LAKE

Many animals and plants live together in and around a lake.

A lake is fed by a river or stream.

Soil and water plants provide homes for insects, birds, fish and other animals.

Frogs, snails and fish eat water plants.

Land animals drink water.

Birds eat plants, insects, fish and frogs.

LASER

A laser is a device that produces a ray of light. The laser's narrow ray of light is very strong.

SEE ALSO
• Light • Satellite

Ordinary light is made up of the colours of the rainbow. Each light wave is a different wavelength.

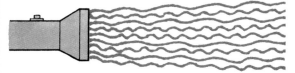

A laser produces light with waves that are all the same. They rise and fall together. This makes the laser's narrow ray very powerful.

HOW A LASER IS USED

Laser beams have many uses.
• Drilling a tiny hole in a diamond.
• Cutting through hard steel.
• Helping doctors in delicate operations.
• Relaying television and telephone signals.
Scientists are working to find new ways to use lasers.

◄ HOLOGRAMS

A hologram is a photograph made with laser light. A hologram looks three-dimensional.

LATITUDE AND LONGITUDE

SEE ALSO	• Earth • Equator • Map • Measurement

Latitude and longitude are lines drawn on maps. Latitude and longitude lines give the position of any place on the Earth.

LINES OF LATITUDE

Latitude lines are the imaginary lines on globes or maps that run around the Earth parallel to the equator. They measure how far north or south a place is from the equator. Lines of latitude are called parallels of latitude.

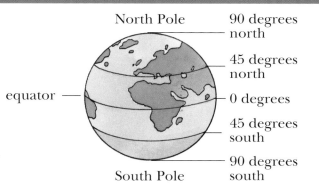

LINES OF LONGITUDE

Longitude lines are the imaginary lines running from the North Pole to the South Pole. Lines of longitude are called meridians of longitude. They measure how far east or west a place is from the Greenwich meridian.

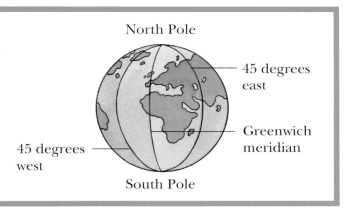

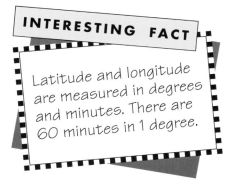

INTERESTING FACT

Latitude and longitude are measured in degrees and minutes. There are 60 minutes in 1 degree.

◀ Sailors and pilots use latitude and longitude to find the location of ships and aeroplanes.

LEAF

SEE ALSO
• Flower • Forest • Plant
• Tree

A leaf is a living thing.
Most plants have leaves.
A leaf makes food for a plant.

PARTS OF A LEAF

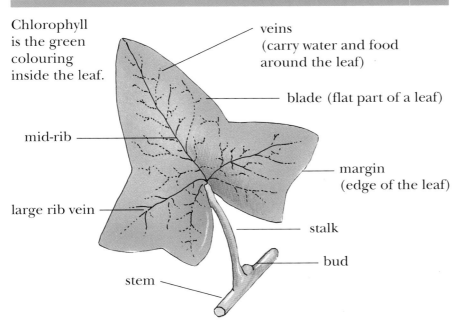

Chlorophyll is the green colouring inside the leaf.

veins (carry water and food around the leaf)

blade (flat part of a leaf)

mid-rib

margin (edge of the leaf)

large rib vein

stalk

bud

stem

HOW A LEAF MAKES FOOD FOR A PLANT

• Each leaf contains chlorophyll which makes the leaf green.
• Chlorophyll traps the Sun's energy in the leaf. The leaf uses the Sun's energy to turn carbon dioxide from the air and water into food.
• This is called photosynthesis.

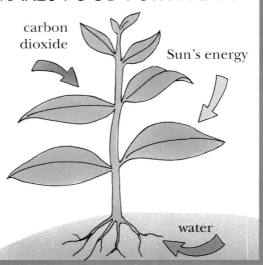

carbon dioxide

Sun's energy

water

KINDS OF LEAVES

Most leaves are green. They come in many different shapes and sizes.

• Pine trees have needle-like leaves.

• Waterlilies have flat leaves which float on water.

• Some plants have climbing leaves.

• Tulip leaves store food for the plant.

EVERGREEN TREES

Evergreen trees do not lose their leaves all at once. As leaves die, new ones grow.

AUTUMN LEAVES ▶

A tree that loses its leaves in autumn is a deciduous tree. The water supply is shut off to the leaves. This makes them lose their green colour. The leaves turn orange, red and yellow. In spring, new leaves grow from buds.

LEAVES FOR FOOD

Leaves provide food for people and animals. Some leaves are used for medicine.

EUCALYPTUS ▼ LEAVES

Some plants such as eucalyptus trees have flat leaves which hang. Only the edges face the Sun. This helps the plant save water.

LIBRARY

SEE ALSO • Book • Newspaper • Paper • Printing

A library is a place where books are kept. People use libraries to gain knowledge and find information. A library also lends books to people to read and enjoy in their leisure time.

CHILDREN'S LIBRARY

A children's library has lots of books that are fun and interesting to read. There are also other materials such as toys, games, compact discs, magazines and posters.

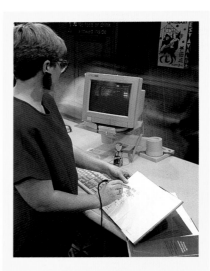

LIBRARIANS

Librarians work in libraries.

• They choose and buy books for the people who visit the library.

• They arrange books and materials on shelves so library users can find them easily.

• They prepare catalogues so library users can find the books they are looking for.

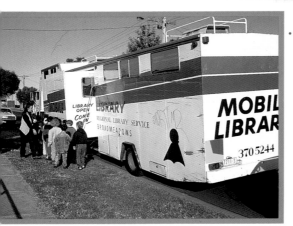

MOBILE LIBRARIES

A mobile library is set up in a large van which can be driven to different places. It provides library services to people who cannot get to their local library.

Libraries keep many different things.

books

magazines

newspapers

pamphlets

photographs

computerized information

databases

CD-ROMs

records

videos

paintings

maps

compact discs

puzzles

toys

games

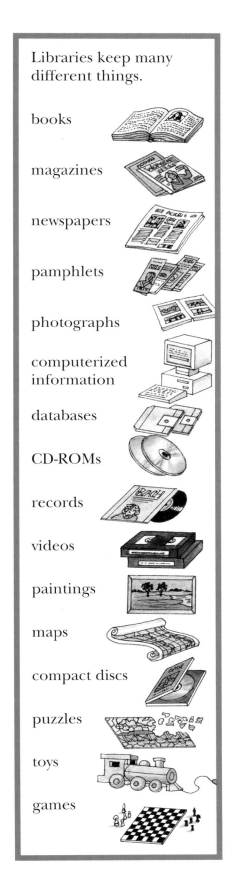

The Library of Congress in Washington DC, USA, is one of the largest libraries in the world. It has about 84 million different items in its collection.

LIFE CYCLE

SEE ALSO • Amphibian • Fish • Flower • Insect • Mammal • Reptiles

All living things have a life cycle. Some living things have simple life cycles. Others have many different stages in their life cycles.

HUMAN LIFE CYCLE

Humans, like all mammals, grow from an egg which has been fertilized. The baby grows inside the mother's body for 40 weeks until it is born.

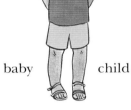

baby   child   teenager   adult

MAMMALS

A mammal begins life inside its mother. It is born live. Young mammals, such as these rabbits, feed on their mothers' milk. They are cared for by their parents until they can find their own food.

When they are born, young animals such as horses, dogs and cats look like their parents, but are smaller in size.

SALMON

Salmon live in the sea but breed in rivers. They swim upstream to lay their eggs. Many die shortly after laying their eggs.

A FROG'S LIFE CYCLE

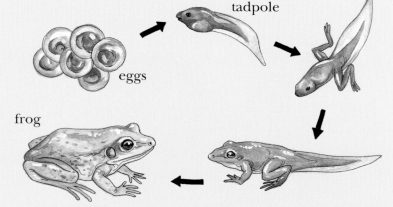

Frogs lay their eggs in water. Tadpoles hatch from the eggs. Tadpoles do not look like frogs. As they grow, they slowly change into frogs.

INSECT LIFE CYCLES

Most insects go through major changes in their life cycles. At each stage, they look very different.

• Some insects, such as the mosquito, have four stages in their life cycles.

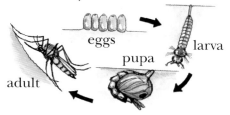

• Insects, such as dragonflies and grasshoppers, have three stages in their life cycles.

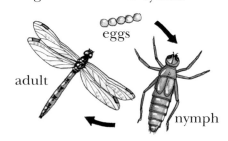

PLANTS

Plants grow from seeds.

• Some plants cannot begin to grow until the seed has passed through a bird's or an animal's body.

• Bees are needed to pollinate some plants before the seed can begin to grow.

LIGHT

SEE ALSO
• Colour • Laser • Rainbow
• Sun

Light is a kind of energy. The Sun is the main source of light on Earth. People have invented other ways of making light, such as electricity.

LIGHT AND LIFE

Plants use the Sun's light to make food. Plants provide food for all other living things.
- Some animals eat plants. Others eat plant-eating animals.
- Bacteria and fungi feed on dead animal and plant matter.

SHADOW

Light can pass through some things, but not others. When light cannot pass through an object, a shadow is cast. The shadow is where no light falls.

SPEED OF LIGHT

Light travels faster than anything else in the Universe. Light travels in a straight line at a speed of 300 000 kilometres each second. Light travels from the Sun to the Earth in eight minutes. The Sun is 150 million kilometres from Earth.

KINDS OF LIGHT

The Sun does not shine all the time, so people have invented other ways of making light. Long ago, people used light from fires and burning torches. Then, candles, and oil and gas lamps were used. Today, electricity is used to provide light.

fire   torch   candle

HEAT CAN CAUSE LIGHT

When the filament in an electric light bulb is heated, it creates light. When you turn on a switch, electric currents travel along wires to the bulb. The electric currents make the filament hot.

The filament glows because it is very hot.

Electricity goes along these wires.

socket

BENDING LIGHT (REFRACTION)

Light rays travel in straight lines. Some things such as glass, air and water make light rays bend. This is refraction.

1. Put a coin in a cup. Move back until you can no longer see the coin.

2. Now add water. Can you see the coin?

REFLECTION

Light rays bounce off things they cannot pass through. This is reflection. A mirror works because of reflection.

RAINBOWS ▶

Light is made up of the seven colours of the rainbow.

oil and gas lamp

electric light

neon light

fluorescent light

laser light

LIGHTHOUSE

SEE ALSO • Boat • Radar • Ship

A lighthouse is a tall tower. Lighthouses warn people at sea that land is near or that dangerous seas are close by.

PARTS OF A LIGHTHOUSE

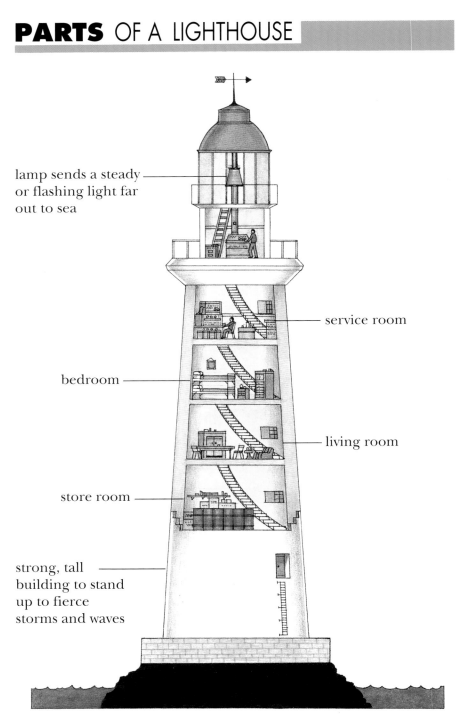

lamp sends a steady or flashing light far out to sea

service room

bedroom

living room

store room

strong, tall building to stand up to fierce storms and waves

EARLY LIGHTHOUSES

In the past, lighthouses were operated by a keeper. The lighthouse keeper lived in or near the lighthouse to look after the lamp.

A LIGHTHOUSE KEEPER'S WORK

- Polishing reflecting mirrors for the lamp.
- Lighting the wick for the lamp.
- Replacing oil used by the lamp.
- Cleaning soot from the windows.
- Rescuing sailors and passengers from shipwrecks.

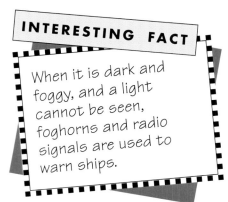

INTERESTING FACT

When it is dark and foggy, and a light cannot be seen, foghorns and radio signals are used to warn ships.

MODERN LIGHTHOUSES

Modern lighthouses send out signals automatically. These lighthouses can operate without keepers. Electric motors provide the power to light the lamp. They are replacing old lighthouses.

SIGNALS

- Each lighthouse has its own pattern of beams or flashes of light.
- This lets navigators at sea know which lighthouse they can see.
- Navigators use the signals to find their ship's position at sea.

DAY MARKER ▶ PATTERNS

Some lighthouses have patterns of checks and stripes. Sailors can then tell one lighthouse from another in the daytime.

WHERE LIGHTHOUSES ARE BUILT

at ports or harbours

on headlands

on rocks

LION

SEE ALSO • Animal • Cat • Jaguars and Leopards • Mammal

A lion is a large wild animal. It is a fierce and strong animal, and has a very loud roar. It is a member of the cat family.

PARTS OF A LION

Average length: 2.8 metres
Average height: 90 centimetres
Average weight: 160 to 180 kilograms

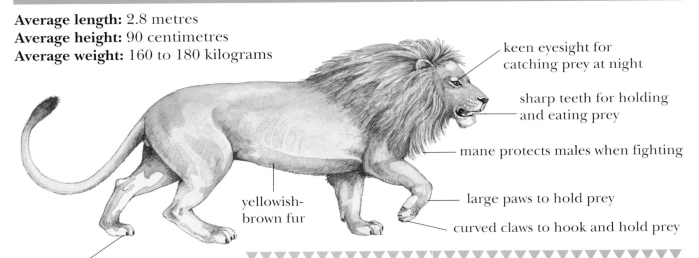

keen eyesight for catching prey at night

sharp teeth for holding and eating prey

mane protects males when fighting

large paws to hold prey

curved claws to hook and hold prey

yellowish-brown fur

claws retract for walking softly

A LION'S MANE

A male lion has a shaggy mane around its head. A lioness is smaller and does not have a mane.

FOOD

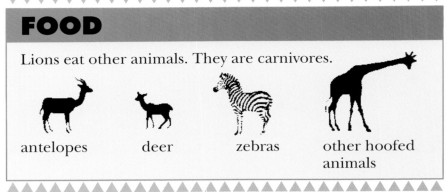

Lions eat other animals. They are carnivores.

antelopes   deer   zebras   other hoofed animals

WHERE LIONS LIVE

● **Africa**
■ **North-west India**

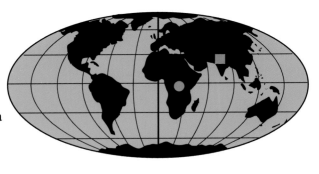

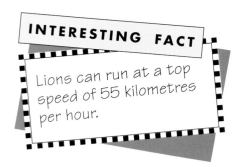

INTERESTING FACT

Lions can run at a top speed of 55 kilometres per hour.

PRIDE OF LIONS

Lions live in family groups called prides. There can be 10 to 35 lions in a pride. They roam on open, grassy plains.

PROTECTED ANIMALS

In the past, many people have hunted lions. Today, lions are protected in India. In Africa, lions live on reserves. Reserves are protected areas.

Lions from a pride hunt in separate places. Usually, the lioness is the hunter. All members of the pride share the catch. Lions eat every three to four days. They kill only when they are hungry. ▼

HOW LIONS LIVE

• Lions spend up to 20 hours a day sleeping and resting.

• Usually two to three cubs are born in a litter. They are blind and helpless at birth. At first, the cubs feed on milk from their mother. At about two months, they eat their first meal of meat.

• Lions can live for up to 25 years.

LIZARD

SEE ALSO • Alligator • Reptiles • Snake • Turtles and Tortoises

A lizard is a reptile. It has a dry, scaly body. Some lizards look like snakes. Others look like a snake with four legs. There are many different kinds of lizards.

PARTS OF A LIZARD

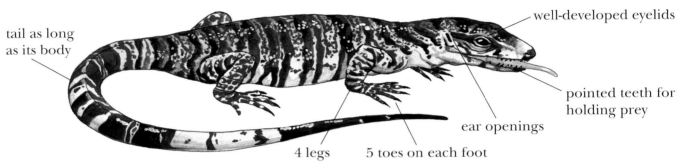

tail as long as its body

well-developed eyelids

pointed teeth for holding prey

ear openings

4 legs

5 toes on each foot

Length: 3 centimetres to 3 metres

WHERE LIZARDS LIVE

Most lizards live in hot countries. Lizards that live in cold countries sleep through the cold winter months.

LEGLESS LIZARDS

Legless lizards are only found in Australia and New Guinea. They have small scale-like flaps instead of legs.

FOOD

Different kinds of lizards eat different foods.

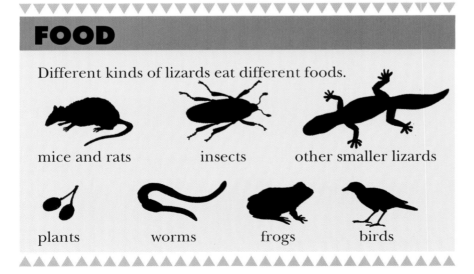

mice and rats

insects

other smaller lizards

plants

worms

frogs

birds

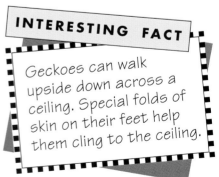

INTERESTING FACT

Geckoes can walk upside down across a ceiling. Special folds of skin on their feet help them cling to the ceiling.

HOW LIZARDS LIVE

• A lizard is a cold-blooded animal. It cannot keep its body temperature constant. It lies in the Sun to keep warm.

• Lizards shelter under rocks, fallen trees and bark. They hide in trees, in grass or on the ground.

• Most lizards lay eggs. Some lizards give birth to live young after the eggs have hatched in their body. The young lizards look after themselves from birth.

• A lizard's skin moults in pieces. A snake moults its whole skin in one piece.

LIZARDS' TAILS

Many lizards can drop their tails when in danger from an enemy. The wriggling tail tricks the enemy, and the lizard escapes. Later, the lizard grows another tail.

A RUNNING ▶ LIZARD

The Australian frill-necked lizard can run on its back legs. This lizard hisses when in danger and raises the frill around its neck.

◀ KOMODO DRAGON

The komodo dragon is the largest lizard. It is three metres long. It is only found on four small Indonesian islands and is protected by law.

LUNGS

SEE ALSO • Blood • Human Body • Nose • Skeleton • Skin

Lungs are organs used for breathing. Amphibians, fish, reptiles, birds and mammals have lungs. Blood takes oxygen from the air in the lungs.

PARTS OF THE LUNGS

Human beings have two lungs, a left lung and a right lung. They look like pink sponges.

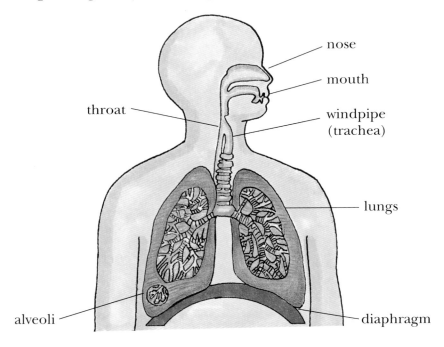

The lungs are made of millions of tiny cup-shaped air sacs called alveoli.

The diaphragm is a strong muscle that divides the chest and abdomen.

INTERESTING FACT

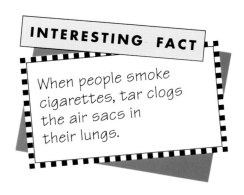

When people smoke cigarettes, tar clogs the air sacs in their lungs.

BREATHING IN

When we breathe in, the lungs stretch like balloons. Air carrying fresh oxygen rushes down to the lungs.

lungs inflated

diaphragm contracted

BREATHING OUT

When we breathe out, we push air out of our lungs. The air takes with it the carbon dioxide waste from the blood.

lungs deflated

diaphragm relaxed

MACHINE

SEE ALSO • Invention • Robot • Wheel

A machine is an object that helps us to do work. It can make work easier. A machine usually has moving parts.

SIMPLE MACHINES

All machines are made up of one or more of these six simple machines.

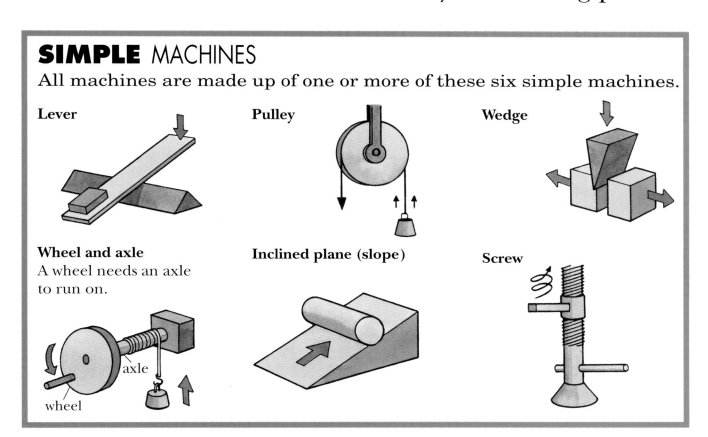

Lever

Pulley

Wedge

Wheel and axle
A wheel needs an axle to run on.

axle

wheel

Inclined plane (slope)

Screw

Machines need energy to make them work. Oil, electricity, water, wind and the Sun can produce energy to make machines work.

MACHINES IN FACTORIES ▶
Machines in factories are made up of many simple machines.

LEVERS
A lever can help you to move something.

MAGIC

SEE ALSO • Games • Hobby

Magic is a way of doing something that looks impossible. A magician is a person who can perform tricks.

PERFORMING MAGICIANS ▼

Magicians perform tricks for groups of people. Some magicians joke and talk while performing. Others perform in silence. Anyone can learn to perform magic tricks. To perform in front of an audience, you must practise a lot. Costumes and make-up can help to make your magic act successful.

A magician can make pulling ▲ a rabbit out of a hat seem easy.

MAGIC PROPS

You can learn a few tricks using simple props such as coins, playing cards or matches.

You can also use magic props such as linking rings, silk scarves and flowers that pop out of a stick.

THE MAGIC CIRCLE CODE

Magicians have a magic circle code. They do not tell people the secret of their tricks.

MAGNET

SEE ALSO
• Telephone • Television

A magnet is a piece of metal such as iron or steel that can pull other pieces of metal towards it. Metals that stick to magnets can also become magnets.

KINDS OF MAGNETS

Magnets come in different shapes and sizes.

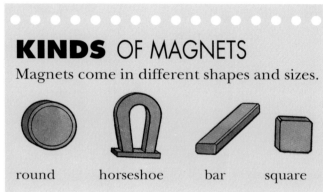

round   horseshoe   bar   square

MAGNETS ARE USEFUL

Magnets are used inside many machines. They are used to make motors work.

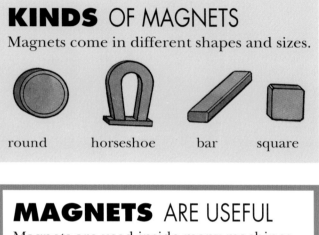

television   telephone   computer

compact disc player   car

MAGNETIC FIELDS ▶

A magnetic field is the area around a magnet that is affected by its pull. It is an invisible force. The stronger the magnet, the stronger the magnetic field.

MAGNETIC POLES

The ends of a magnet are called the poles. This is where the pull of the magnet is strongest.

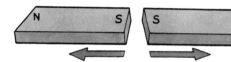

• Poles which are the same push each other away.

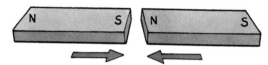

• Opposite poles pull towards each other.

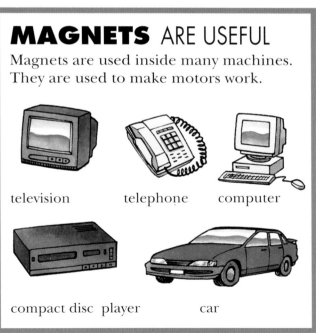

MAMMAL

A mammal is an animal that feeds on its mother's milk when it is young. There are over 4000 different kinds of mammals.

SEE ALSO • Animal • Marsupial • Hair • Vertebrate

MAMMALS
- Mammals give birth to young.
- They produce milk to feed their young.
- They are warm-blooded animals.
- Mammals have hair, fur or wool on their bodies.

THREE GROUPS OF MAMMALS

Monotremes are mammals that lay eggs. The young animals grow inside the eggs. When the eggs hatch, the young feed on their mother's milk.

platypus   echidna

Marsupials are mammals that have a pouch. The young are born partly developed. They crawl to their mother's pouch where they finish growing.

kangaroo   koala

Placental mammals give birth to fully developed young.

dolphin   bat   goat   human being

MAMMOTH

SEE ALSO • Dinosaur • Fossil

A mammoth was a large woolly mammal that lived long ago. Mammoths lived in times that were much colder than today. They belonged to the same family as elephants.

PARTS OF A HAIRY MAMMOTH

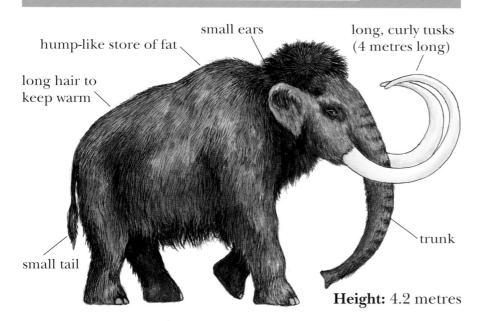

hump-like store of fat

small ears

long, curly tusks (4 metres long)

long hair to keep warm

small tail

trunk

Height: 4.2 metres

FOOD

plants

grasses

leaves

INTERESTING FACT

The frozen bodies of mammoths have been found by scientists in Siberia. They were perfectly preserved.

HOW MAMMOTHS LIVED

Mammoths lived in groups called herds. They were hunted by sabre-toothed tigers, wolves and cave people. Pictures found on cave walls show cave people hunting mammoths.

MAMMOTH FOSSILS

The oldest known remains of mammoths have been found in India. They date from four million years ago. Remains of mammoths have also been found in North America and Siberia. Mammoths died out about 10 000 years ago.

MAP

SEE ALSO
• Latitude and Longitude
• Road • Satellite

A map is a drawing of all or part of the Earth.
Maps can help you find a place.

PARTS OF A MAP

Maps are flat. They are drawn as if you are looking down from above.

Maps are drawn to scale. The area shown on a map is much larger than the map. A scale is used to draw things small enough to fit on a map.

Grid lines are drawn on a map to divide it into squares. Letters are used along the vertical lines which run down the map. Numbers are used along the horizontal lines which run across the map. This makes it easier to find places. You can find the monkey bars at B1.

The key explains the symbols used on a map.

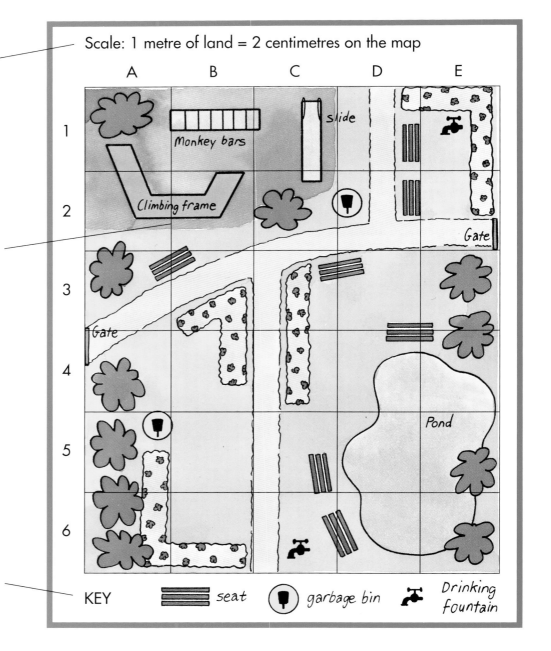

Scale: 1 metre of land = 2 centimetres on the map

Monkey bars
Climbing frame
slide
Gate
Gate
Pond

KEY   seat   garbage bin   Drinking fountain

KINDS OF MAPS

There are many different kinds of maps.

Political maps show countries and their borders and cities.

Physical maps show continents, rivers, mountains, plains and other land features.

AERIAL PHOTOGRAPHS ▶

People who make maps are called cartographers. They use aerial photographs and measurements of places to draw maps to scale.

SATELLITE MAPS

Satellites in space take photographs of the Earth's surface. These photographs are used to make maps.

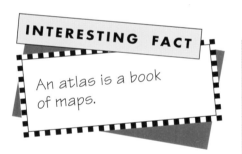

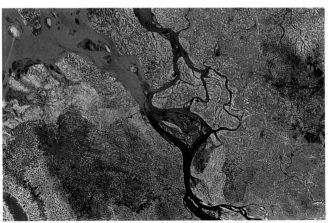

MARSUPIAL

A marsupial is a mammal with a pouch. Young marsupials are very small and undeveloped at birth. They crawl to their mother's pouch where they stay until they are well developed.

SEE ALSO
• Animal • Kangaroo • Koala
• Mammal • Vertebrate

The American opossum stays in its mother's pouch for about two months. When an opossum grows too large for its pouch, it rides on its mother's back.

A young kangaroo crawls into its mother's pouch and attaches itself to one of her teats.
It feeds on its mother's milk until it is big enough to look after itself.
It usually stays in the pouch for about 90 days.

KINDS OF MARSUPIALS

There are over 250 kinds of marsupials.

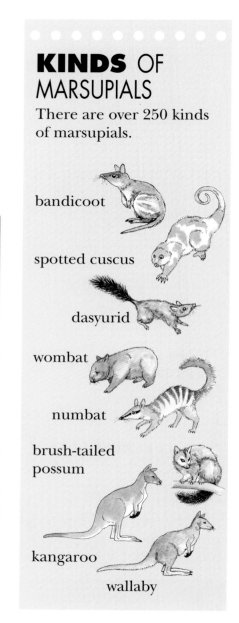

bandicoot

spotted cuscus

dasyurid

wombat

numbat

brush-tailed possum

kangaroo

wallaby

WHERE MARSUPIALS LIVE

● Australia
■ New Guinea
◆ North America
★ South America

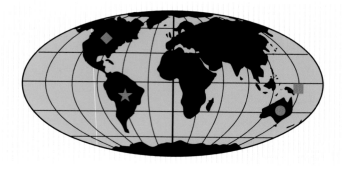

MARSUPIAL
MEASUREMENT

| SEE ALSO | • Calendar • Clock |
| | • Days of the Week • Fraction |

MEASUREMENT

Measurement is the way we find out the size or quantity of something. When you measure something, you find out how many standard units are in it.

HISTORY

The ancient Egyptians used a system of measurement based on the human body.

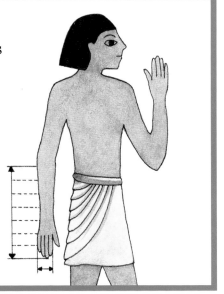

7 palms = 1 cubit

4 digits = 1 palm

MEASUREMENT SYSTEMS

Most countries use the metric system for measuring. The metric system divides things into units of ten.

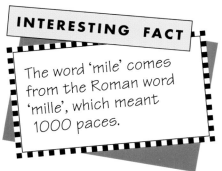

INTERESTING FACT

The word 'mile' comes from the Roman word 'mille', which meant 1000 paces.

MEASURING UNITS

- Millimetres, centimetres, metres and kilometres measure length.
- Grams, kilograms and tonnes measure weight.
- Seconds, minutes and hours measure time.

SOME MEASURING TOOLS

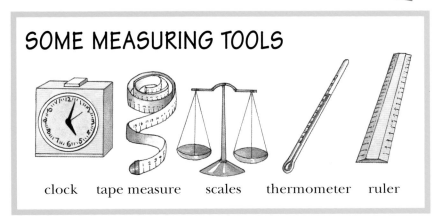

clock   tape measure   scales   thermometer   ruler

45

METAL

SEE ALSO • Minerals • Mining • Rock

Metal is a hard material. Metals make up a large part of the Earth's crust. Metals carry electricity and heat. They can be made into wire, hammered or rolled into shapes.

WHERE METALS ARE FOUND IN THE WORLD

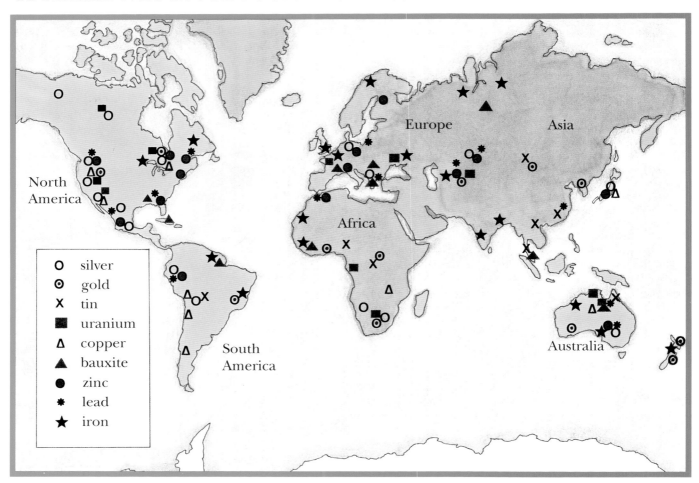

O	silver
⊙	gold
✕	tin
■	uranium
△	copper
▲	bauxite
●	zinc
✳	lead
★	iron

HISTORY

Copper was the first metal to be found. It was made into bronze by mixing it with tin. Bronze tools replaced stone knives and axes.

46

USES OF METAL

Metals are used to make many of the things we use.

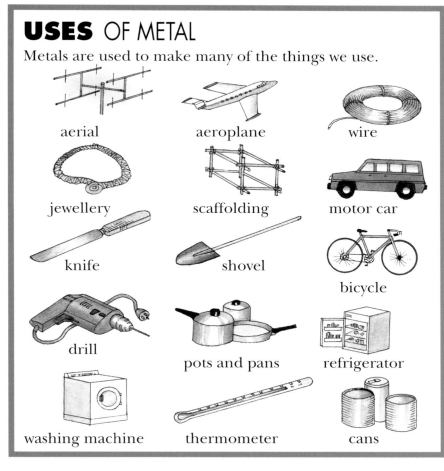

aerial   aeroplane   wire

jewellery   scaffolding   motor car

knife   shovel

bicycle

drill   pots and pans   refrigerator

washing machine   thermometer   cans

METAL ORE

Copper, silver and gold are pure metals which can be dug straight from the ground. Most other metals have to be taken from rock.

Most metals are found in rocks. Rocks that contain metals are called ores. The rocks are dug from the ground and processed to remove the metals.

RECYCLING METALS

Metals can be recycled. Recycling metals reduces waste and is cheaper than processing metal ores.

METAL ALLOYS

An alloy is a mixture of different metals. Bronze is an alloy. It is made from copper and tin. Many statues are made from bronze. A mould is made in the shape of a statue. The alloy is melted and poured into the mould. When the liquid cools, it is the shape of the statue.

INTERESTING FACT

Although most metals are solid, the metal mercury is liquid at room temperature.

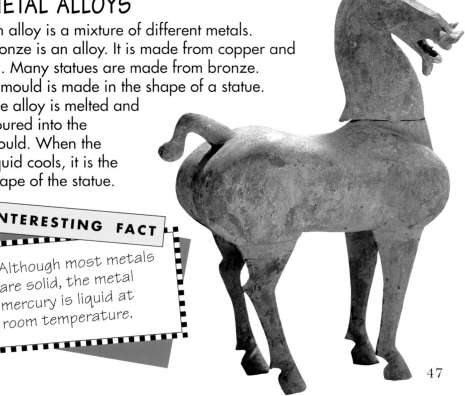

METEOR

SEE ALSO • Earth • Sun • Universe

A meteor is a small piece of metal or stone that flies through space. We can only see meteors when they enter the Earth's atmosphere.

When the Earth moves around the Sun, it collides with millions of meteors. Meteors travel at great speeds.

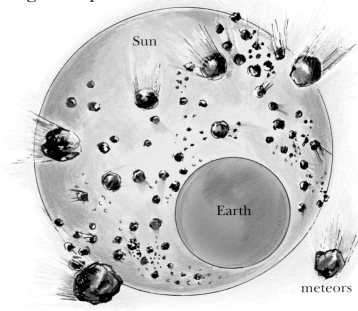

Sun

Earth

meteors

SHOOTING STARS

A shooting star is a meteor that enters the Earth's atmosphere. As they fall to Earth, most meteors heat up and burn away to nothing.

SIZE OF METEORS

Meteors vary in size. Some are like huge boulders; others are tiny bits of dust.

METEORITES

Sometimes, large meteors reach Earth. They are called meteorites. A crater is a large hole made by a meteorite in the Earth's surface.

MINERALS

SEE ALSO • Metal • Mining • Quarry • Rocks

Minerals are non-living materials found in the Earth's surface. All rocks contain minerals. Minerals are dug out of the ground.

GRANITE ▼
Granite is a rock. It contains bits of the minerals hornblende, feldspar, quartz and mica.

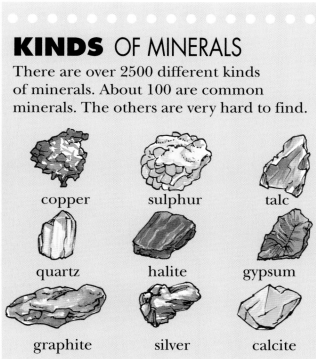

KINDS OF MINERALS
There are over 2500 different kinds of minerals. About 100 are common minerals. The others are very hard to find.

copper sulphur talc
quartz halite gypsum
graphite silver calcite

USES OF MINERALS

Graphite is a mineral used in pencils to make pencil lead.

Talc is the softest mineral. It is used to make talcum powder.

A diamond is a mineral. It is the hardest mineral.

Rock salt is the mineral halite.

SOIL
Soil contains tiny bits of minerals from crushed rock. Minerals help plants to grow.

SEA SALT
The salt in the sea is a mixture of minerals. Water dissolves minerals in rocks on land. The dissolved minerals are washed into the sea.

49

MINING

SEE ALSO • Gas • Metal • Minerals • Oil • Quarry • Rocks

Mining is the way we take the things we need from the Earth. Mining provides people with tin, gold, silver, coal, iron ore, oil and natural gas.

OPEN-CAST MINING ▶

Open-cast mining is used if the minerals are found close to the Earth's surface. The soil containing the minerals is lifted from the surface.

UNDERGROUND MINING

When the minerals are deep below the Earth's surface, they are mined in underground tunnels. In South Africa, gold is mined nearly three kilometres below the Earth's surface.

UNDERWATER MINING

Underwater mining is used to reach minerals which are found in the seabed. Special mining rigs are built in the sea to mine oil and natural gas.

| SEE ALSO | • Invertebrate • Octopus
• Oyster • Snail |

MOLLUSCS

Molluscs are a large group of animals which have a single muscular foot. All molluscs have soft bodies and no backbones.

MOLLUSCS AND SHELLS

• Many molluscs have shells which protect their soft bodies.
• Shells come in many shapes, sizes, colours and patterns.
• Some molluscs, such as squid, have shells inside their bodies.
• All molluscs' shells are made of limestone.

INTERESTING FACT

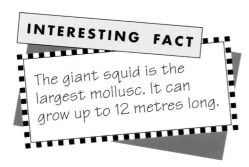

The giant squid is the largest mollusc. It can grow up to 12 metres long.

SOME KINDS OF MOLLUSCS

There are many different kinds of molluscs. Some molluscs live on land; many live in the sea.

Chitons have a shell made of eight plates.

Bivalves have ▶ two shells that are joined by a muscle. A clam has two shells.

Cephalopods have internal shells. A squid has an internal shell. ▼

Gastropods ▶ have a single shell. Sea snails and garden snails have a single shell.

MONEY

SEE ALSO
• Bank • Gold • Paper
• Shop

Money is the coins and paper notes people use to buy things.

COINS

Coins are made of metal and last a long time.

BANK NOTES

Bank notes are made of paper. They represent an amount of money. Some bank notes are made of plastic. Coins and paper notes are known as cash.

CHEQUES AND CREDIT CARDS

Cheques and credit cards can be used instead of cash.

HISTORY ▶

Long ago, people did not use money to buy goods. Instead, they exchanged goods. This is called bartering.

MONEY AROUND THE WORLD

Every country has its own money which looks different and has a different name.

America
dollars and cents

England
pounds and pence

Australia
dollars and cents

France
francs and centimes

Japan
yen

China
yuan, jiao and fen

COINS

Long ago, coins were made of gold and silver. Today, cheaper metals are used to make coins. Coins are stamped to show how much they are worth and which country they belong to.

MONKEY

SEE ALSO
• Animal • Ape • Mammal
• Rain Forest

A monkey is a furry animal. Monkeys have long fingers and toes which they can use to grasp things. Most have tails which they can use to swing in trees.

PARTS OF A SPIDER MONKEY

Length: 51 to 89 centimetres

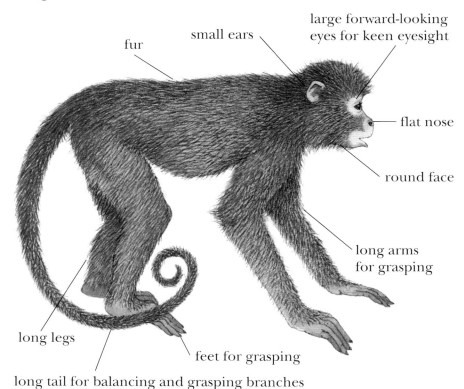

fur

small ears

large forward-looking eyes for keen eyesight

flat nose

round face

long arms for grasping

long legs

feet for grasping

long tail for balancing and grasping branches

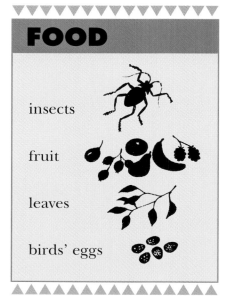

FOOD

insects

fruit

leaves

birds' eggs

INTERESTING FACT

Monkeys belong to the same group of animals as apes and human beings.

WHERE MONKEYS LIVE

Most monkeys live in tropical rain forests.
- ● **South America**
- ■ **Central America**
- ◆ **Africa**
- ★ **Asia**
- ▲ **South-western tip of Europe**

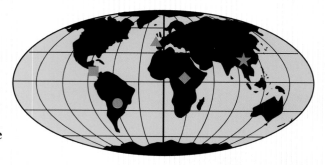

HOW MONKEYS MOVE

Most monkeys live in forests, swinging and leaping among the trees. On the ground, monkeys move around on their four limbs. Monkeys can stand on two feet and grasp things with their hands.

HOW MONKEYS LIVE

- Most monkeys live in family groups.
- Usually, the female monkey gives birth to one baby at a time. The young monkey feeds on its mother's milk. The female carries the young monkey until it can look after itself.
- Most monkeys are active during the day and sleep at night.

KINDS OF MONKEYS

There are many different kinds of monkeys. They can be divided into two main groups – New World monkeys and Old World monkeys.

New World monkeys live in Central and South America.
- They live in trees.
- They have tails.
- They have 36 teeth.
- They have short noses with nostrils wide apart.

Spider monkeys belong ▶ to the New World group of monkeys.

Old World monkeys live in Africa and Asia.
- Most live on the ground.
- Most have no tails.
- They have 32 teeth.
- They have long noses with nostrils close together.

Baboons are ground- ▶ dwelling monkeys. They belong to the Old World group of monkeys.

MONTHS OF THE YEAR

SEE ALSO
• Calendar
• Days of the Week

Months are used to measure time. There are 12 months in one year.

HOW MANY DAYS?

This rhyme helps you remember how many days there are in each month.

Thirty days hath September
April, June and November;
All the rest have thirty-one,
Except for February alone,
Which has but twenty-eight days clear,
And twenty-nine in each leap year.

JANUARY

January is the first month of the year. It is 31 days long. It was named after the Roman god Janus who had two faces.

FEBRUARY

February is the second month of the year. It is 28 days long. Every fourth year, February is 29 days long. This is a leap year. It was named after Februo, a Roman festival of purification.

MARCH

March is the third month of the year. It is 31 days long. March was named after Mars, the Roman god of agriculture and war.

APRIL

April is the fourth month of the year. It is 30 days long. April comes from the Latin word *Aprilis* which means to open.

MAY

May is the fifth month of the year. It is 31 days long. May was named after the Greek goddess Maia.

JUNE

June is the sixth month of the year. It is 30 days long. June was named after Juno, the chief of all the Roman goddesses.

MONTHS OF THE YEAR

JULY

July is the seventh month of the year. It is 31 days long. July was named after the Roman emperor Julius Caesar.

AUGUST

August is the eighth month of the year. It is 31 days long. August was named after the Roman emperor Augustus Caesar.

SEPTEMBER

September is the ninth month of the year. It is 30 days long. September comes from the old Roman word *septem* which means seven. In an older Roman calendar, it was the seventh month.

OCTOBER

October is the tenth month of the year. It is 31 days long. October comes from the old Roman word *octo* which means eight. In an older Roman calendar, it was the eighth month.

NOVEMBER

November is the eleventh month of the year. It is 30 days long. November comes from the Roman word *novem* which means nine. In an older Roman calendar, it was the ninth month.

DECEMBER

December is the twelfth month of the year. It is 31 days long. December comes from the Roman word *decem* which means ten. In an older Roman calendar, it was the tenth month.

MOON

SEE ALSO • Astronaut • Satellite • Spacecraft • Tide

The Moon travels around the Earth. It is the Earth's nearest neighbour in space. There is no air, wind or water on the Moon. Nothing grows or lives there.

◄ The Moon has a rough surface with many craters. It is about one quarter the size of the Earth.

INTERESTING FACT

Footprints left on the Moon by astronauts will never change. This is because there is no wind on the Moon to blow them away.

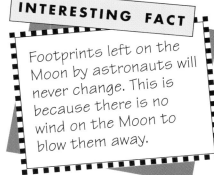

HISTORY

From Earth, the Moon looks patchy. Before people could study the Moon with telescopes, they thought a man lived on the Moon. Some people thought the Moon was made of cheese.

MOON ROCKS

Astronauts have brought back soil and rocks from the Moon. These show that the Moon is 4.6 billion years old, the same age as the Earth.

◀ TRAVELLING TO THE MOON

The Moon is the first place in space visited by people from Earth. A rocket journey from Earth to the Moon and back again takes about six days.

GRAVITY ON THE MOON

The force of gravity on the Moon is six times weaker than that on the Earth. This means you can jump six times higher on the Moon.

INTERESTING FACT

The same side of the Moon always faces the Earth.

INTERESTING FACT

On the Moon, astronauts use radios to talk to each other. This is because there is no air to carry soundwaves.

PHASES OF THE MOON

It takes about 29 days for the Moon to travel around the Earth. During this cycle, the Moon has eight phases where it looks as though it changes shape.

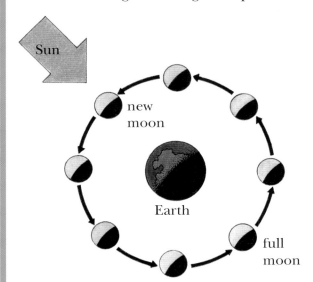

Sun

new moon

Earth

full moon

This is because the Moon has no light of its own. It reflects the Sun's light. As the Moon travels around the Earth, different parts of the Moon are lit by the Sun.

MOTOR CAR

SEE ALSO
• Motorcycle • Pollution
• Road • Transport

A motor car is a vehicle with four wheels and an engine. It is driven by a person and can carry passengers. People use motor cars to travel from one place to another.

PARTS OF A MOTOR CAR

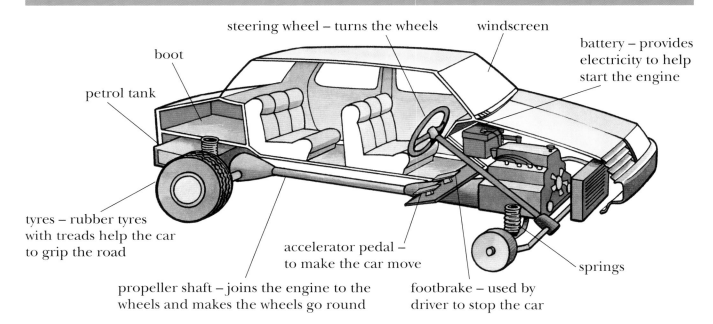

steering wheel – turns the wheels

windscreen

battery – provides electricity to help start the engine

boot

petrol tank

tyres – rubber tyres with treads help the car to grip the road

accelerator pedal – to make the car move

springs

propeller shaft – joins the engine to the wheels and makes the wheels go round

footbrake – used by driver to stop the car

HOW AN INTERNAL COMBUSTION ENGINE WORKS

- The engine makes the wheels go round.
- Petrol and air burn inside each cylinder.
- This moves the pistons up and down inside the cylinders, which turns the crankshaft.
- The crankshaft turns the propeller shaft.
- The propeller shaft makes the wheels go round.

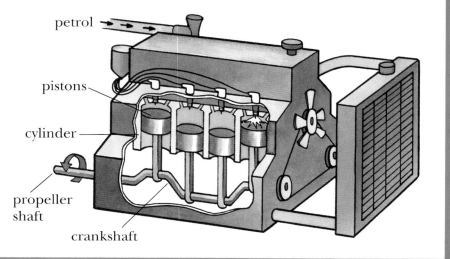

petrol

pistons

cylinder

propeller shaft

crankshaft

HISTORY ▶

In 1886, the German engineers, Karl Benz and Gottlieb Daimler, invented the internal combustion engine to drive cars. The early cars were handmade and very expensive.

◀ HENRY FORD

Henry Ford's motor company set up the first assembly line. Cars could be mass-produced quickly and cheaply. In 1908, the Ford Motor Company made the Model T Ford, the first mass-produced car.

ROAD TRAFFIC ▶

Today, there are more cars on the road than ever before. This has caused problems such as air pollution and traffic accidents.

MOTORCYCLE

SEE ALSO • Pollution • Road • Transport

A motorcycle is a vehicle with two wheels and an engine. People ride motorcycles to travel from one place to another.

PARTS OF A MOTORCYCLE

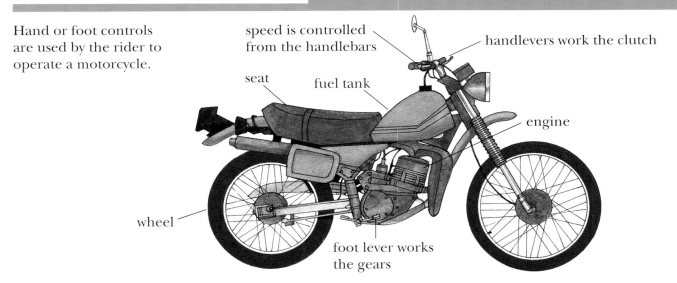

Hand or foot controls are used by the rider to operate a motorcycle.

speed is controlled from the handlebars

handlevers work the clutch

seat

fuel tank

engine

wheel

foot lever works the gears

HISTORY

Gottlieb Daimler built the first motorcycle in 1885. He fitted one of his internal combustion engines to a wooden bicycle frame.

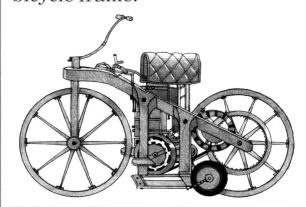

KINDS OF MOTORCYCLES

There are many different kinds of motorcycles. Trail bikes can be ridden over rough country, up hills and across streams.

MOUNTAIN

A mountain is a large mass of earth that is higher than the surrounding land.

| SEE ALSO | • Earth • Volcano |

Mount Fuji is the highest mountain in Japan. It was made when a volcano poured molten rock on to the surface of the Earth. Mount Fuji is 3776 metres above sea level.

UNDERSEA MOUNTAINS

Some islands, such as Hawaii, are the tops of undersea mountains and volcanoes.

FAMOUS MOUNTAINS

The highest mountain on Earth is Mount Everest. It is 8848 metres above sea level. In 1953, the first people to climb to the top of Mount Everest were Edmund Hillary and Tenzing Norgay.

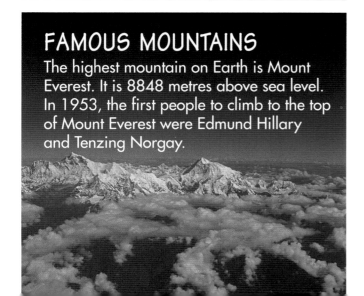

HOW MOUNTAINS ARE MADE

Most mountains are formed by movement in the Earth's crust.

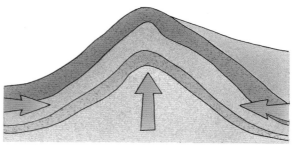

• Fold mountains are made when two plates push against each other. This causes the Earth's crust to fold and crumple like a piece of paper.

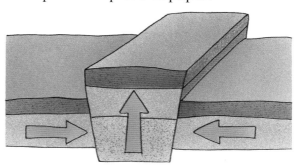

• Block mountains are made when two land masses move towards each other and squeeze up the land in between.

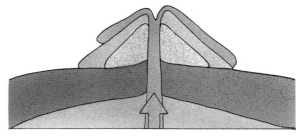

• Volcanic mountains are made by molten rock escaping from deep down in the Earth and piling up on the Earth's surface.

MUSIC

| SEE ALSO | • Ballet • Bell • Orchestra • Xylophone |

Music is the sound you make when you sing or play a musical instrument. Music can be written using symbols called notes.

MUSICAL ▶ PERFORMANCES

Musicians, singers and conductors work together to perform music for an audience.

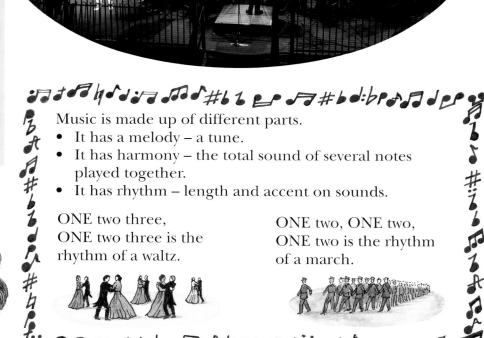

KINDS OF MUSIC

There are many different kinds of music.

- Classical
- Rock
- Jazz
- Folk
- Opera

Music is made up of different parts.
- It has a melody – a tune.
- It has harmony – the total sound of several notes played together.
- It has rhythm – length and accent on sounds.

ONE two three,
ONE two three is the
rhythm of a waltz.

ONE two, ONE two,
ONE two is the rhythm
of a march.

◀ COMPOSERS

Composers are people who make up music and write it down. Beethoven was a famous German composer who lived from 1770 to 1827.